Morris County MEMORIES

VOLUME III ~ THE 1970s '80s & '90s

presented by

Copyright© 2004 • ISBN: 1-932129-83-9
All rights reserved. No part of this book may be reproduced, stored in a retrieval system or transmitted in any form or by any means, electronic, mechanical, photocopying, recording or otherwise, without prior written permission of the copyright owner or the publisher.
Published by Pediment Publishing, a division of The Pediment Group, Inc.   www.pediment.com   Printed in Canada

Table of Contents

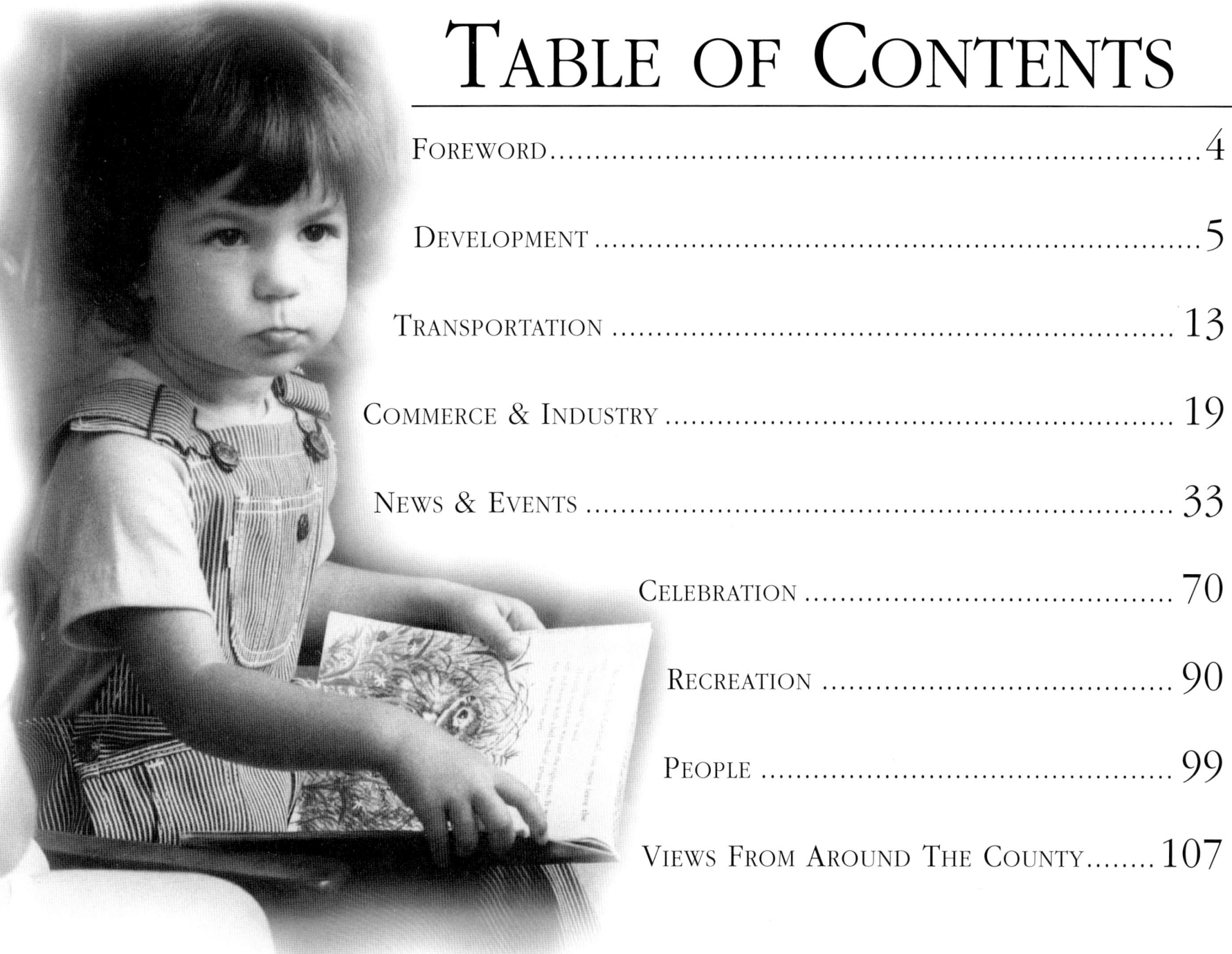

Foreword 4

Development 5

Transportation 13

Commerce & Industry 19

News & Events 33

Celebration 70

Recreation 90

People 99

Views From Around The County 107

FOREWORD

Perhaps none of the volumes in this pictorial series of memories of Morris County has given us as much pleasure to produce as this one, covering the years 1970–1999. Many of us at the Daily Record remember these things happening. Photographers remember taking the photos. Reporters remember writing the stories. Editors remember the headlines and the mad dashes to meet deadline on what seemed the most important stories ever. We remember the energy crisis and the outrage and fear people felt when service stations began running out of gas. We remember the Vietnam War, protests around the Green in Morristown and solemn ceremonies at cemeteries on Memorial Day. We remember HOV lanes. The fight over the right to die that was secured in the Karen Ann Quinlan case. Hot days swimming at Lake Hopatcong. Long hair. The excitement of winning big games at area high schools. The good and the bad, the enriching and the sad.

This book lets us see and feel the early days in our lives. We see, perhaps better than ever, how we were then, and how things have changed. We see how stories twisted and turned. How what started out one way ended quite differently. How the long hair of the 1970s turned into the short hair at the end of the millennium. How it was newsworthy when gas hit 75 cents a gallon during the energy crisis, which doesn't seem so bad by today's standards.

The Daily Record is pleased to give you these scenes a second time, some 30 years later.

We, ourselves, have changed a lot over the years. Who would have thought in the 1970s, for instance, that the next generation would read us on computers, at dailyrecord.com, over something even stranger called the Internet? What hasn't changed is what we do - bringing you local news and advertising, from Morris County and beyond. It's been our job and our passion since the first issue of the Daily Record on June 25, 1900.

We hope you enjoy Volume III of Morris County Memories. And we hope to be serving you for a lot of years to come.

Walt T. Lafferty
President and Publisher
Daily Record

DEVELOPMENT

These were the years when Morris County wondered if it had grown big enough. By the time of the 2000 Census, it counted 470,212 residents, up 87,000 from 1970. Housing prices were out of sight, averaging $350,000 countywide, and they were double that in some towns. The great interstates, Routes 80 and 287, were given additional lanes but slowed to crawls at rush hour.

Condominiums, townhouses and McMansions sprouted in the most unlikely places. And while Montville was the fastest-growing town in the 1990s, most of the growth occurred in the once-rural western part of the county, where farms and other developable land disappeared almost in the blink of an eye. Many towns imposed their own open space taxes on property sales, generating money to buy and keep other land open for the future. Some down-zoned and required 5-acre minimum lot sizes in areas previously zoned for two acres. That may have reduced the number of potential new homes, but it also drove up home prices.

The great westward push for cheaper land farther from New York continued. Increasingly, Morris County workers drove home to sleep in Sussex or Warren counties or, farther yet, across the Delaware River into Monroe County, Pa.

Two big commercial developments were in at the start of this period. Rockaway Townsquare, the county's first big enclosed mall, opened along Route 80 in Rockaway Township in 1977. It's still the largest, most concentrated retail space in the county. About the same time a block-long section of old stores near the Green in Morristown was torn down to make way for an urban renewal project centered around Headquarters Plaza, a 15-story, 260-room hotel. It opened in 1983, bringing a glitz not seen elsewhere in the Revolutionary War-era town.

The 2000 Census also showed a big change in the nature of Morris County's population: sharp growth in the number of people who said they were Hispanic or Latino. Countywide, the total was put at 36,626, or nearly 8 percent of the county's population. In Dover they constituted 58 percent of the population. In Morristown, 27 percent.

Construction workers are framed by a cinderblock wall at the building site of Town Square Village, Rockaway, April, 1992. *Colleen Harrington photo*

DEVELOPMENT

Park Theater was demolished to make way for urban renewal in Morristown, October 15, 1970. *Daily Record staff photo*

Senior citizens project construction, Dover, January 24, 1973. *Daily Record staff photo*

Buildings along Speedwell Avenue and Spring Street in Morristown had to be demolished to make way for urban renewal, January 31, 1971.
John Bell photo

Work continues on Spring Street during Morristown's urban renewal, May 2, 1975. *John Bell photo*

DEVELOPMENT

Charles Wilkerson, left, and Kevin Peterkin watch the construction at Speedwell Avenue in Morristown, March 2, 1976. *Michael Gaffney photo*

Parking structure being constructed in Morristown, October 31, 1980.
R.S. Townsend photo

A crane lifts construction materials atop one of the office towers in the Headquarters Plaza project in Morristown, July 22, 1982. *Dave Schemelia photo*

Construction at St. Clare's Hospital nears completion in Denville, December 30, 1982.
Dave Schemelia photo

A cluster of condos along Route 10 in Succasunna, January 22, 1989.
Daily Record staff photo

DEVELOPMENT

The foundations of what would later become Headquarters Plaza in Morristown, as seen on June 8, 1980, from the 10th floor of the 1776 Building next door. Small shops and other buildings in the area, bounded by Speedwell Avenue to the left and Spring Street on the right, were demolished for the project in the 1970s. The 15-story $38 million Headquarters Plaza Hotel opened on November 28, 1983. An adjoining mall housing 55 shops would open several weeks later. *Robyn Craig photo*

Susan Gulbach of Rutherford and Mike Cebula of Nutley wait for a real estate company sales office to open in Montville so they can buy a townhouse, February 7, 1992. There were more prospective buyers than units, so a lottery was held.
Chris Pedota photo

Archeologist Bill Sandy of Newton examines a piece of white, salted-glazed stoneware from approximately 1740-1775 that he found at the construction site of a park and ride lot along Route 46 in Parsippany, June 25, 1997. *Bob Karp photo*

Ed Lenik studies an article found in the ground near Sand Shore Road in Mount Olive, April 30, 1992, as Ron Dupont and Rick Patterson sift through dirt. They were conducting random diggings about every 50 feet searching for artifacts. *Karen Fucito photo*

DEVELOPMENT

Workers patch Route 22 in Montville as a new sewer line is installed for a nearby development, March 3, 1997. *Dawn Benko photo*

A "McMansion" at Reservoir Ridge Estates in Mendham, September 23, 1999. *Chris Pedota photo*

A "McMansion" at Reservoir Ridge Estates in Mendham Township, September 23, 1999. *Chris Pedota photo*

TRANSPORTATION

During the last years of the 20th Century, it sometimes seemed Morris County would burst at the seams along two bisecting interstate highways, Routes 80 and 287. Rush hours became inescapable battlegrounds braved by tens of thousands of motorists. They crawled along the interstates. They crawled along the four-lane highways surrounding them. They cracked their knuckles, and bumpers, at clogged-up intersections.

The state of New Jersey, with the lure of millions of dollars from the federal government, added an extra lane to each interstate and called them HOV lanes, reserved during rush hours for high occupancy vehicles (as in two or more people). Complaints were deafening. The HOV lanes were largely empty while the old ones remained clogged. State legislators and the federal government heard the cries, and in 1999 the HOV designations were removed. Best yet, the state didn't have to repay the federal government the cost of building the lanes in the first place.

Sound walls, meanwhile, at a reported cost of $1 million a mile, went up along both roads to shield encroaching neighborhoods from traffic noise.

In 1992 Gov. Jim Florio opened the 20.5 mile link of Route 287 north of Boonton. A year later, he opened the 8-mile extension of high-speed Route 24, which for years ended at Chatham, west to Route 287. Opposition by less developed towns farther west nixed the highway's planned extension to Mendham, and the proposed route was taken off state planning maps.

NJ Transit took a little more traffic off the road with a new route called Midtown Direct in 1996. Riders could now get on the train in Dover, Morristown, and elsewhere to be delivered directly to Midtown Manhattan. Previously they had been forced to change trains in Hoboken for a trip under the Hudson River. Ridership swelled, and the number of Hoboken trains shrank.

Aerial view of Ledgewood Circle, Route 46, Roxbury, 1990. *Daily Record staff photo*

TRANSPORTATION

Route 80 construction at Cherry Hill Road, Parsippany, May 20, 1971. Route 80, Morris County's main east-west connector route, stretches 2,909 miles from New York to San Francisco. The first of the 68 miles in New Jersey was completed in 1973 just east of the Delaware River. The last, in Morris County, opened in 1973. Total cost in New Jersey: $345 million. *John Bell photo*

Workers pave a northbound lane on Route 287 between Routes 10 and 46, July 14, 1976. Route 287 was conceived as a bypass around New York and, in Northern New Jersey, a bypass around Route 202. Construction began at the southern end in 1958. Crews moved into Morristown after great opposition and even civil disobedience (townspeople sat on the blades of the invading bulldozers) in 1965. For years the highway ended in Montville before a 20.5-mile missing link was completed north of the town in 1993. *Bruce Crawford photo*

Triborough Road interchange in Florham Park and Chatham Borough. Route 24 passes in the middle of these round-abouts, 1981. *Daily Record staff photo*

Barrier construction on Route 287 near Morris Avenue in Morristown, September 11, 1974. *Bruce Crawford photo*

Traffic cruises west past a 55 mph sign along Route 80, May 16, 1986. The speed limit, cut during the energy crisis, was increased to 65 mph in Parsippany in 1998. *Stan Godlewski photo*

TRANSPORTATION

Construction of a bridge carrying Mount Hope Road over Route 80 in Rockaway, May 18, 1985. *John Bell photo*

Aerial view of the construction of Route 287, Montville, 1989. *Robert Sciarrino photo*

Carpenter Stephanie Smith of Clark works on a Route 287 culvert in Montville, August 31, 1990. *John Bell photo*

A crowd celebrates the grand opening of Rockaway Townsquare, August 12, 1977. *John Bell photo*

Mall-goers enjoy food and music at Rockaway Townsquare, August 12, 1977. *Eric Ward photo*

The opening party at the two-level mall, August 12, 1977. *John Bell photo*

COMMERCE & INDUSTRY

Youngsters enjoy an afternoon at the arcade at the Bertrand Island amusement park at Lake Hopatcong, May 25, 1977. *Michael Gaffney photo*

Riders on the Aero-Jet at Bertrand Island, May 25, 1977. *Michael Gaffney photo*

Bertrand Island amusement park closes in September 1983. *Daily Record staff photo*

The amusement park at Bertrand Island, Mount Arlington, after it closed in September 1983. It opened in 1915, and for generations of youngsters, it was the place to have fun in the summer. *Daily Record staff photo*

Mount Arlington firefighters extinguish a fire at Bertrand Island, January 23, 1986.
Stan Godlewski photo

Pat Falcetano dismantles the roller coaster at Bertrand Island, April 4, 1986.
Daily Record staff photo

COMMERCE & INDUSTRY

A Seeing Eye instructor, students and dogs train at a crosswalk near the Morristown Post Office, August 31, 1977. The Seeing Eye has trained its guide dogs on Morristown streets for years. *Daily Record Staff Photo*

Angie, Kim Wollinger's 4-H project for the Seeing Eye, waits patiently in a truck that will take her to a new life, November 12, 1979.
Mike Grant photo

Seeing Eye dog breeder Rob Wickman tends puppies at his Mendham Township farm, March 5, 1979. *Michael Gaffney photo*

Dinna Brash and her dog, Tish, avoid sidewalk obstacles in Morris Township as instructor Peter Jackson observes, January 21, 1979. *Daily Record staff photo*

David Loux of the Seeing Eye crosses an intersection followed by a Daily Record reporter led by another dog, November 29, 1982. *Robyn Craig photo*

COMMERCE & INDUSTRY

Instructor Dave Johnson of the Seeing Eye walks Smiddy around the Morristown Green, March 10, 1999. In the background is the First Presbyterian Church.
Daily Record staff photo

Physicist Pierre Petroff with "Ulysses," an early computer, which he conceptualized and built at AT&T Bell Labs in Murray Hill, July 1986. *Stan Godlewski photo*

Telephone poles at a Bell Labs facility in Chester Township, October 5, 1989. Poles of different types would be erected at the farm, then monitored for how they performed over the years. *Karen Fucito photo*

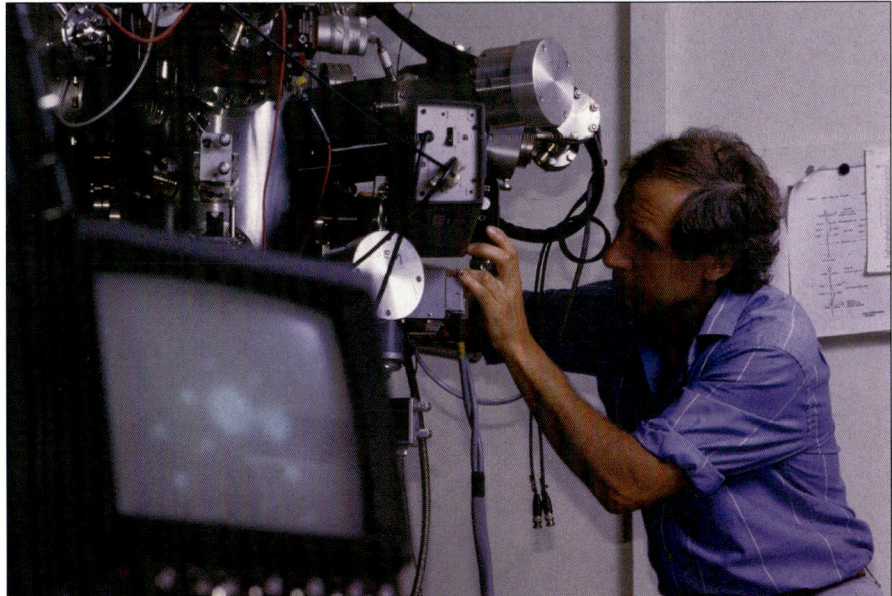
Petroff at the controls of "Ulysses," July 1986. *Stan Godlewski photo*

Robin M. Gilman, a researcher at Warner-Lambert Co., a major pharmaceutical company headquartered in Morris Plains, uses computer-based thermal imaging to take pictures of temperature emitted by a subject, January 22, 1989. *Daily Record staff photo*

COMMERCE & INDUSTRY

Office construction in Rockaway Township, August 25, 1988. *Karen Fucito photo*

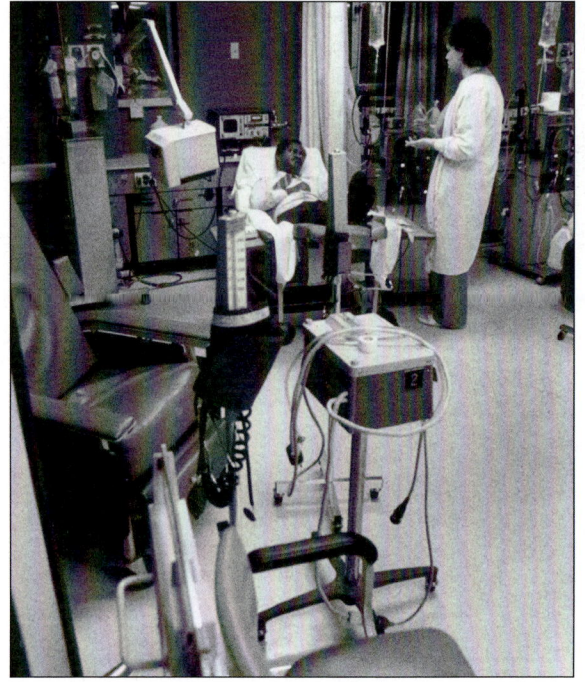

Giovanni Sandioris trims Christmas trees at Coviello Brothers', a garden center, in Madison, December 20, 1988. *Daily Record staff photo*

Monitored by registered nurse Eileen Cullim, a patient undergoes hemodialysis at Morristown Memorial Hospital, January 3, 1985. *Stan Godlewski photo*

1987 photo of Sandoz Pharmaceuticals (now Novartis) located at the corner of Route 10 East and Ridgedale Avenue in East Hanover. *Chris Pedota photo*

Bob Erles puts up an 80th anniversary sign at the family-owned Epstein's department store in Morristown, November 15, 1992. *Daily Record staff photo*

Shoppers at Epstein's department store, near the Green in Morristown, 1991. The store opened in 1912 and was the town's grand dame of retailing at the end of the century. In 2004, Epstein's closed, to be replaced by a smaller store and hundreds of housing units. *Daily Record staff photo*

COMMERCE & INDUSTRY

Dawn Balut, a 22-year employee at BASF (she is a legal assistant), has been through six moves with the company. She herself moved to Byram Township seven years ago in anticipation of BASF moving to Mount Olive, October 3, 1994.
Karen Fucito photo

Firefighters and police during training exercise at the Morris County Academy, March 27, 1990. *Daily Record staff photo*

Training at the Morris County Fire Fighters and Police Training Academy in Parsippany, March 27, 1990. *Daily Record staff photo*

Steve Honickman, a mechanical engineer at Picatinny Arsenal, the Army weapons development center in Rockaway Township, gives the media a rundown of a Patriot missile warhead, January 25, 1991. The surface-to-air missile was a star in the Gulf War that month. *Chris Pedota photo*

Capt. Thomas Bryant rides aboard an M1A1 Abrams Tank during a media tour of some of the armaments developed at Picatinny, January 1991. *Chris Pedota photo*

Spc. Owen Bigler, a gunner, atop the Army's newest weapon, a self-propelled Howitzer, at Picatinny Arsenal, May 23, 1991. The field artillery had a crew of four. *Karen Fucito photo*

COMMERCE & INDUSTRY

Warner-Lambert Co. pharmacist Lynda Williams works on the drug Mitrostat, a nitroglycerin tablet that is dissolved under the tongue for treatment of acute angina, January 13, 1992. The drug was involved in several Food and Drug Administration recalls to correct manufacturing and testing problems. *Karen Fucito photo*

Taste tester Alex Johnson in a tasting booth at Warner-Lambert's product testing lab, Morris Plains, August 14, 1990. *Tim Farrell photo*

Warner-Lambert headquarters in Morris Plains, August 23, 1993. Pfizer acquired the pharmaceutical company in 2000 after a 3-month takeover battle, creating the largest U.S. drugmaker. *Daily Record staff photo*

News & Events

The time was like any other 30 years, full of news, big news.

None, perhaps, was bigger than the precedent-setting, 1976 U.S. Supreme Court decision that allowed Julia and Joseph Quinlan of Roxbury to disconnect a respirator from their comatose, brain dead daughter. The machine had kept her alive, but in a chronic vegetative state, for 399 days. For the first time, the court recognized a person's right to die. Karen Ann Quinlan passed away, on June 11, 1985, unaware of the national debate surrounding her plight.

If the Quinlan decision seemed to affect few, the energy crisis affected everyone, right in the gut. Oil price increases by producing nations in the Middle East caused energy prices to skyrocket everywhere. Motorists, fearing shortages, caused runs on gas stations, some of which went empty or rationed purchases. Public officials turned off street lights to save money. Conservation became a watchword. The country fell into recession. Unemployment blossomed.

There were big fires, big crimes, big trials and small political corruption. There was the resignation of President Nixon and the governorship of Tom Kean. There was the Vietnam War. There were protests against everything – from nuclear energy to abortion. Signs of NIMBY (Not In My Backyard) mindsets were everywhere. There were big snows, big explosions and big elections.

These events were not so long ago. Many of us still remember them. Even now, receding into the background, they were big news for any day.

Morristown Police Lt. Sam Perrillo maintains peace during a Vietnam War protest, May 8, 1970. *Tim Manning photo*

Vietnam War protest in Morris County, May 6, 1970. *Daily Record staff photo*

Linda Struble collects money for a trip to Washington to protest the Vietnam War, May 8, 1970. *Tim Manning photo*

Vietnam War protest on the Green in Morristown, May 6, 1970, two days after four protesting students were shot and killed by the National Guard at Kent State University in Ohio. They were protesting U.S. bombing in Cambodia. *Tim Manning photo*

Joanne Chesimard headed into the Morris County Jail, December 30, 1973.
Daily Record staff photo

The Chesimard Trial

Joanne Chesimard, a leading figure in the Black Panther movement of the 1960s who joined the extremist Black Liberation Army, was one of the most notorious inmates of the Morris County Jail. She was there for just a short time, awaiting trial in New Brunswick for killing a state trooper during a traffic stop on the New Jersey Turnpike in 1973. Security was tight: Only 20 members of the public and 20 reporters were allowed to watch jury selection.

The killing occurred on May 2, 1973, when Chesimard and two friends were stopped on the turnpike by two troopers. While being questioned, she and the driver allegedly opened fire with automatic pistols, striking one trooper twice in the chest and the other in the shoulder. Then an additional two bullets were fired execution style into Trooper Werner Foerster's head, killing him. Chesimard was shot twice by troopers and arrested five miles from the scene.

After a six-week trial, she was found guilty of first-degree murder and sentenced to life in a New Jersey maximum-security prison. But it didn't last long. In 1979, she made a daring daylight escape from the Edna Mahan Correctional Facility for Women in Clinton, when four of her visitors took a guard and a prison driver hostage. She fled to Cuba, where Fidel Castro granted her political asylum. She remains New Jersey's most wanted criminal.

JoAnne Chesimard supporters on the Green in Morristown, January 11, 1974. *Bruce Crawford photo*

JoAnne Chesimard supporters, January 11, 1974. *Bruce Crawford photo*

NEWS & EVENTS

Firefighters back away from thick smoke billowing from the front of the United Methodist Church on the Green in Morristown during an enormous fire, January 20, 1972. *Tim Manning photo*

Stephen Frick, president of the United Methodist Church youth fellowship, stacks hymnals in a shopping cart after the fire, Morristown, January 20, 1972. *Tim Manning photo*

The United Methodist Church, which was dedicated in 1870, is torn down after the fire, which left only the bell tower and front wall standing, July 17, 1973. It was reconstructed the following year. *John Bell photo*

A couple keep their coats on to stay warm during lunch at the Wedgewood Inn during the energy crisis, Morristown, February 8, 1977. *Daily Record staff photo*

The Grand Union supermarket in Morristown complied with the governor's orders to help save energy by lowering the temperature, January 29, 1977. *Bruce Crawford photo*

A house on Brownstone Place in Mount Olive damaged by a tornado that touched down in Flanders, May 30, 1973. *John Bell photo*

Morris County residents in line at a state unemployment office, February 1, 1977. New Jersey's unemployment rate that month was 10.7 percent – the eighth consecutive month in double digits, in large part because of the energy crisis. *John Bell photo*

Karen Ann Quinlan

Her name never should have been known to those outside her family and small circle of friends. Karen Ann Quinlan, however, became a household figure when she slipped into a coma that set off a national debate that culminated in a landmark Supreme Court decision on a terminally ill patient's right to die.

Quinlan, 21, was the first modern icon of the right-to-die debate. She collapsed at a Sussex County restaurant in 1975 after apparently swallowing alcohol and tranquilizers at a party. Doctors saved her life, but she suffered brain damage and lapsed into a "persistent vegetative state," an irreversible coma. Her parents, Joseph and Julia Quinlan of Landing, waged a much-publicized legal battle for the right to remove her life support machinery. They took their case to the New Jersey Supreme Court, which in a landmark decision, sided with the parents. In a final twist, Quinlan kept breathing after her respirator was disconnected. She remained in a coma for almost 10 years at Morris View nursing home in Morris Township until her death of pneumonia in 1985 at the age of 31.

The Quinlan's case produced the first judicial ruling in the United States to permit the removal of life-sustaining medical treatment from a permanently incompetent patient. And it played a role in the development of the living will and advance directive, and in the establishment of ethics committees in hospitals throughout the United States.

Joseph and Julia Quinlan besieged by the media after a court hearing in Morristown, October 20, 1975. *John Bell photo*

Joseph and Julia Quinlan at a press conference, June 10, 1976, three weeks after their daughter was removed from a respirator. *John Bell photo*

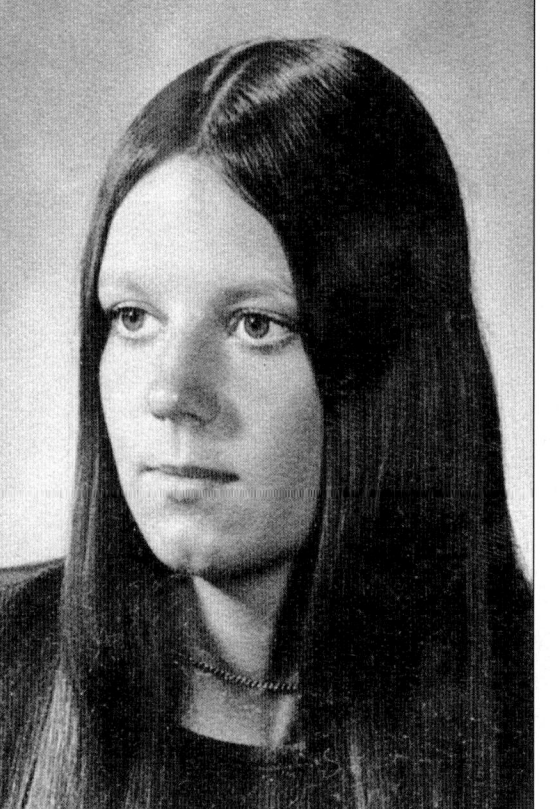

Karen Ann Quinlan's portrait as a high school senior, September 15, 1975.

The Quinlans answer a barrage of questions from the media, April 1, 1976, after the New Jersey Supreme Court ruled their daughter could be disconnected from a respirator. *John Bell photo*

Karen Ann Quinlan's casket is carried out of Our Lady of the Lake Church, Mount Arlington, June 14, 1985. She died of pneumonia three days earlier at Morris View nursing home in Morris Township, nine years after being removed from a respirator.
Daily Record staff photo

Julia and Joseph Quinlin mourn their daughter's death, June 14, 1985.
Daily Record staff photo

Gas Hard to Get

The energy crisis, combined with a deep recession, ruled life in Morris County and across the nation. In 1973, the Organization of Petroleum Exporting Countries placed an embargo on oil going to the United States. Prices doubled. Some service stations ran out of gas, and motorists had to wait in line to get as little as 5 gallons. "People are definitely running scared. They're sucking up all the gas we have," said Ed Sagendorf, owner of a station in Chatham Township.

President Nixon ordered thermostats in federal facilities set at 68 degrees. Public officials ordered elevators used less. Streetlights were turned off. Attending PTA meetings became a chilling experience, as Morris County school superintendents turned back thermostats in schools immediately after students left each day. In most cases, that meant a temperature of 58 degrees. The state mandated that winter vacations be extended by three days, also to save fuel. And Parsippany Mayor Henry Luther warned Daily Record readers that the area would face power outages throughout the winter.

That was just in 1973. It took years for the crisis to end.

Peter Andruskiewicz of Boonton Township had just enough gas in his tank to get back home, so he didn't take any chances wasting fuel on the gas line. Attendants at a Shell station in Denville had warned him they might run out of gas before his turn came up to fill up, June 29, 1979.

Lloyd Shannon photo

A driver waits it out in a gas line along Route 10 in Mountain Lakes, June 24, 1979.
Linda McConnell photo

Mary Arale of Kinnalon still can't see the service station after waiting in a gas line for two hours, June 23, 1979. *Peter Byron photo*

Route 80 sign changed to reflect the times, Roxbury, June 27, 1979. *Stu Davis photo*

During the gas shortage, Ziggy's station on Route 10 stayed open with five-hour days and a $5 limit, June 18, 1979. Approximately 85 cars an hour could get their limit. *Linda McConnell photo*

NEWS & EVENTS

The top of an MG Midget can barely be seen in flood water off Hinchman Avenue in Denville, January 1, 1979. *Daily Record staff photo*

Anti-nuclear protesters climb atop a General Public Utilities sign in Parsippany, on the one-year anniversary of the Three Mile Island (Pa.) nuclear power plant accident. GPU owned the plant. *John Bell photo*

Anti-nuclear demonstrators sit in the driveway of GPU offices, Parsippany, March 28, 1980. *John Bell photo*

An anti-nuclear demonstrator is dragged away after crossing a police line at GPU's Parsippany office, March 28, 1980. *John Bell photo*

NEWS & EVENTS

Mary Kate Vassau of Morristown on a park bench at the Green in Morristown during a smoke-in protest, October 13, 1984. *Scott Keeler photo*

Anti-nuclear demonstrators Bunny and Pete Daubner and their daughter Martina block the main door to the GPU offices. *R.S. Townsend photo*

Anti-draft protesters in front of the Parsippany Post Office, July 27, 1980. *Daily Record staff photo*

Aftermath of the Wharton explosion, January 12, 1984. The explosion and fire destroyed four buildings, including the popular Heslin House hotel-restaurant. Mayor Thomas Beirne estimated damage at $2 million and said it was a miracle no one was killed. *Daily Record staff photo*

Aerial view of downtown Wharton on January 12, 1984, after a late-night gas leak caused two explosions that fueled a five-hour fire in the business district.
Daily Record Staff Photo

Firefighters extinguish flare-ups after the Wharton explosion, January 11, 1984.
Robyn Craig photo

Aftermath of the Wharton explosion and fire, January 12, 1984.
Daily Record staff photo

Some fun out of disaster: The bar from the Heslin House, damaged by the fire, is set up in the snow after the Wharton explosion, January 1984. *Daily Record staff photo*

The Catholic Church of the Assumption in Morristown burns on April 11, 1985. The fire began in a crawl space between the ceiling and the roof when a high-intensity light burned the casing off its wires and ignited old beams. *Daily Record photo*

The Catholic Church of the Assumption's slate roof is dismantled, April 11, 1985. The 1872 structure was repaired and is on the National Register of Historic Places. *Daily Record staff photo*

Firefighters battle the blaze at the Catholic Church of the Assumption on Maple Avenue in Morristown, April 11, 1985. *Daily Record staff photo*

The Catholic Church of the Assumption fire in Morristown in April 1985, caused major damage – the roof caved in. Seven years earlier, the congregation had funded major interior renovations. *Daily Record staff photo*

NEWS & EVENTS

Anti-abortion protester Skip Robokoff holds his 7-month-old daughter at an abortion rights rally on the Morristown Green, August 30, 1989. *Chris Pedota photo*

Circle of Friends Leaders Jailed

The judge called George Jurcsek "a modern day Fagin," then sentenced the spiritual leader of the Circle of Friends on March 13, 1989, to seven years in prison for his part in a loan fraud scheme. His assistant, Mary P. O'Rourke, a co-leader in the secretive group, also got seven years. The pair were convicted in December 1988 of defrauding the state of more than $155,000 between 1979 and 1983.

While operating the defunct Saltz Hotel in Randolph, Jurcsek, 69, and O'Rourke directed 32 members ranging in age from 20 to 30 to apply for state-guaranteed student loans and then to donate the proceeds to the group. Superior Court Judge Marianne Espinosa Murphy compared Jurcsek to the old thief who leads a group of youthful pickpockets in Charles Dickens' classic "Oliver Twist." She pronounced: "The Circle of Friends began as an idealistic venture motivated by youthful idealism. ... But when faced with economic distress, Mr. Jurcsek used his influence over his youthful followers ... to commit a massive fraud."

According to testimony from former member Margaret Hamilton Desaussure of Connecticut, the Circle of Friends was a "cult" of members who pledged their obedience and paychecks to a leader who called outsiders "rats." Jurcsek's philosophy was that the group should be a community readying itself for an "earth catastrophe," which he predicted by the year 2000, she said.

George Jurcsek, spiritual leader of the Circle of Friends, and Mary P. O'Rourke, an assistant, 1987.
Daily Record staff photo

The "M" for a sign that would eventually spell "Macy's" is erected on the department store that had been called Bamberger's since 1949, in Morristown, October 7, 1986. *Glen E. Ellman photo*

Aerial view of the damage caused by the Hercules explosion, Roxbury, June 1989. The plant produced gunpowder for decades. *Daily Record staff photo*

Hercules Explosion

Three early-morning explosions at Hercules Inc., which had been making gunpowder since 1871, rocked Roxbury on June 3, 1989. Eleven workers and three residents were hurt, and the blasts caused more than $1 million in damage to the plant and nearby homes and businesses. Gov. Thomas H. Kean declared a state of emergency.

The triple explosions, which were felt as far as 30 miles away, started in a building used to dry gunpowder. About 50 trees were sheared off at the ground or uprooted. Of the 300 buildings on the 1,200-acre site, four were flattened and many were damaged. Eighty-five percent of the businesses in the township had broken windows and blown-out doors. One man said his 55-gallon fish tank shattered. Another reported that his garage was moved off the foundation. A waitress at the Fireside diner on Route 46 said she "saw black smoke, a yellow mushroom cloud and a fireball. It was like an atomic bomb went off."

It wasn't the first explosion at the plant. More than 50 people were killed in a similar accident on September 12, 1940, as dynamite and gunpowder were made for the war effort. *Daily Record Staff*

Aftermath of the Hercules explosion in Roxbury, June 1989. *Daily Record staff photo*

Glass is replaced at a business damaged by the Hercules explosion, Roxbury, June 1989. *Daily Record staff photo*

Firefighters work to stop flames from spreading from Mead Hall to the library building, which was connected by an overhead roof. *Robert Sciarrino photo*

NEWS & EVENTS

Fire companies battle the blaze that nearly destroyed historic Mead Hall at Drew University, Madison, August 24, 1989. The fire was accidentally started by a contractor finishing renovations. *Robert Sciarrino photo*

The third floor of Mead Hall, Drew University, where most of the fire damage occurred, Madison, August 25, 1989. *Dawn Benko photo*

A cherry-picker is used to clean up Mead Hall after the fire, Madison, August 28, 1989. *Karen Fucito photo*

Reconstruction of Mead Hall at Drew University, Madison, November 30, 1989. The work cost $14 million and took three years to complete. *John Bell photo*

Restoration of fire-damaged Mead Hall, Drew University, Madison, August 24, 1990. *Steve Wliser photo*

NEWS & EVENTS

A young man is stranded in the fast water of the Rockaway River as firemen and rescuers try to get lines to him, May 21, 1989.
Jeanne A. Van Riper photo

Young man after grabbing rescue ropes to get to shore. The current almost took him away, May 21, 1989. *Jeanne A. Van Riper photo*

Baby Mary, a newborn found dead in woods off Mount Pleasant Road in Mendham Township on Christmas Eve, 1984, is buried at St. Joseph's Cemetery, October 25, 1989. She was found by Mendham Township Police wrapped in towels and placed in a plastic bag. How she got there and who left her remain mysteries. *Daily Record staff photo*

Joanne Gonzalez assesses damage from a tornado that claimed a tree in front of her house on Waterloo Road in Budd Lake, November 16, 1989. *Chris Pedota photo*

NEWS & EVENTS

A resident of Riverside Drive in Denville carries the necessary equipment for a flooded basement: a sump pump and PVC piping, May 17, 1990. *Karen Fucito photo*

During flooding in Denville, Benny Squeo Jr. and his brother Vito get around in a rowboat on Riverside Drive, May 18, 1990. *Daily Record staff photo*

Kristine Zimmerman says goodbye to her boyfriend, Cpl. Robert Ellis of Millburn, at Picatinny Arsenal in Rockaway Township, November 27, 1990. He was being deployed to Iraq for the 1991 Gulf War. *Karen Fucito photo*

NEWS & EVENTS

Parsippany Mayor Frank Priore waves to the crowd at the Parsippany Day Parade, May 12, 1990. *Tim Farrell photo*

Priore Starts 5-Year Prison Term

With all but two districts reported, Parsippany Mayor Frank Priore receives congratulations from Drew Britcher, his Democratic opponent. In the background is Parsippany Police Chief Michael Filippello, November 7, 1989. *Robert Sciarrino photo*

Frank Priore could have been mayor for life, or so said many people in Parsippany. He got things done. He took care of people. He was a regular guy, but flamboyant. He liked people, and they liked him.

Then Priore, mayor for 12 years, was charged in federal court with petty corruption. After a four-month trial in 1994, he was found guilty, along with former Knoll Country Club golf superintendent Donald Mueller, of schemes to get free dental benefits, hotel rooms and bribes from the caterer of the township's two golf course restaurants.

Priore, then 45, denied any wrongdoing at first, but later apologized for his actions. He was sentenced to five years in prison and ordered to pay $5,102 in restitution. On his way into a medium/maximum security facility accompanied by his girlfriend Joyce DeSpirito, whom he married in 1995 while in prison, Priore told reporters: "It's not the best day of my life. I have to go through with it and get this over with." He was released in 1999.

Laura Gallagher of Parsippany and her friend's dog, Max, get the royal treatment from Parsippany Mayor Frank Priore at Parsippany Day, May 15, 1993. *Bob Karp photo*

NEWS & EVENTS

Excavating Combe Fill North in Mount Olive, April 12, 1990. A 65-acre landfill from 1966 to 1978, it became a Superfund site in 1983 and was declared clean in 2004. *John Bell photo*

Dirt being used in remediation is trucked from McNear's Quarry in Hopatcong to Combe Fill South in Chester, August, 1993. *Time Farrell Photo*

June Perry uses a water filtration system in her kitchen April 18, 1989, because of water contamination caused by Combe Fill South, a landfill in Chester and Washington townships from the 1940s to 1981. It was declared a Superfund site in 1983. *Jim Anness photo*

Patricia Reso, wife of kidnapped Exxon International President Sidney J. Reso of Morris Township, pleaded for her husband's safe return, at their home in Morris Plains, June 16, 1992. *Bob Karp photo*

Patricia Reso speaks to the press on the federal courthouse steps after the sentencing of Arthur Seale to life in prison for the kidnapping and murder of her husband, November 30, 1992. Morris County Prosecutor Michael Murphy is to her left. *John Bell photo*

The Sidney Reso Kidnapping

U.S. Attorney Michael Chertoff called it the cruelest crime he had ever investigated. The victim was abducted, shot in the arm, stuffed alive into a coffin-shaped box and dumped in a self-storage locker in Warren County. There he died while two abductors attempted in vain to extort $18.5 million in ransom.

Sidney J. Reso, the president of Exxon International in Florham Park, was the victim. On April 29, 1992, as he attempted to leave his home in Morris Township, a man and a woman, forced him into a van at gunpoint, shooting him in the arm during a scuffle. They stuffed him in the box and hid it in a rented storage locker the size of a small room in Warren County.

On May 3, Reso died. Still, Arthur and Irene Seale sought a ransom. The resulting investigation grew into the largest kidnapping case in U.S. history and involved 300 FBI agents. Finally on June 19, with authorities staking out pay phones all over the county, the Seales were arrested. In their rental car, authorities found two pairs of rubber kitchen gloves, four Eddie Bauer laundry bags, a briefcase with a 1985 Exxon directory marking the home and addresses of the company's top executives, and three .38-caliber slugs. Eight days later Irene Seale led police to a shallow grave her husband dug for Reso in Bass River State Park in the Pine Barrens.

Arthur Seale, a former Hillside police patrolman and Exxon security official, pleaded guilty to kidnapping and murder and was sentenced to life. His wife, in return for helping police find Reso's body, was sentenced to 20 years.

Secure Storage in Washington Township, where Sidney Reso was taken on April 29, 1992, and held in a coffin-shaped box by kidnappers Arthur and Irene Seal, June 30, 1993. *Colleen Harrington photo*

NEWS & EVENTS

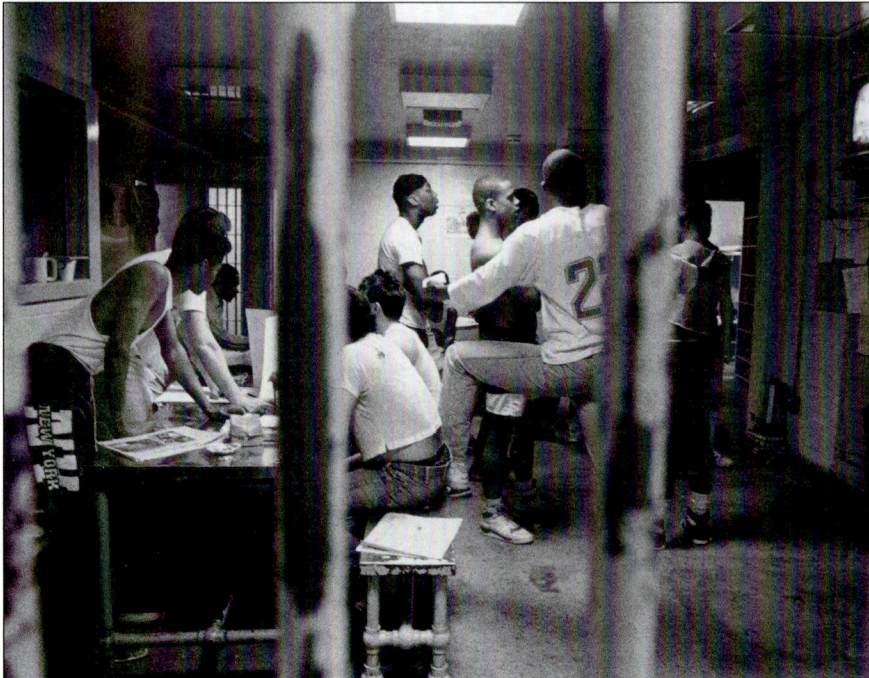

Day room in G-Block was supposed to be a recreational area for 10 inmates, but about 30 were there this day, Morristown, June 6, 1988. *Karen Fucito photo*

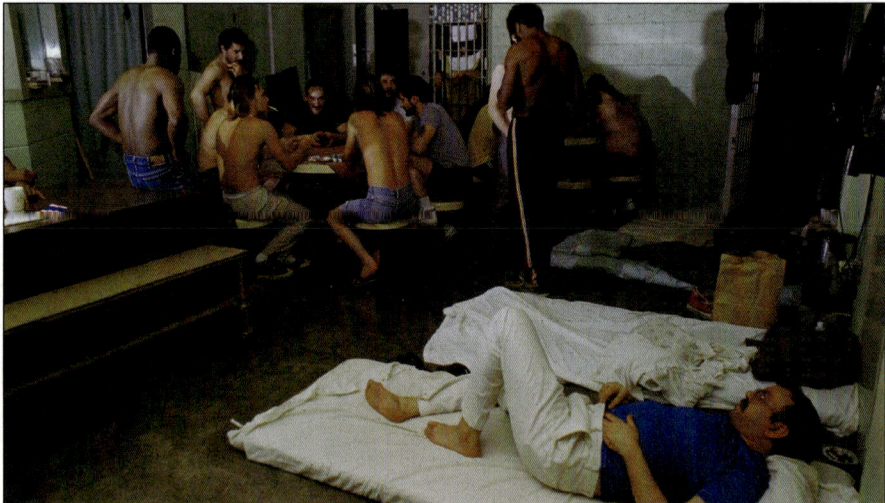

Cell in G-Block at the Morris County jail was supposed to house just one inmate, but overcrowding had three inmates living in this one room, June 6, 1988.
Karen Fucito photo

Overcrowded day room at the Morris County jail in Morristown, 1986. The 60-year-old jail, which was attached to the county courthouse, was replaced by a larger one costing $32 million. *Daily Record staff photo*

Paul Krumbholz wears his opinion on his T-shirt at a meeting to discuss a proposed new Morris County jail. The meeting was held at the Thomas Jefferson School in Morristown, June 23, 1992. *Tim Farrell photo*

Morris County politicians and construction officials applaud work on the new Morris County jail at a topping off ceremony, Morris Township, September 24, 1998. *Chris Pedota photo*

Abortion protesters line Route 46 and Baldwin Road in Parsippany, October 7, 1991. *Daily Record staff photo*

NEWS & EVENTS

Sam Guerra checks the depth of rain-caused floodwater at the intersection of Edith and Curtis streets, Roxbury, September 27, 1994. *Chris Pedota photo*

Pat Ornelas shovels the sidewalk in front of her Washington Street apartment in Morristown after a major snowstorm, January 9, 1996. *Bob Karp Photo*

Jordan Weitberg, an attorney, lectures Denville Police Department officers and some of their spouses about investing their money after a pool of 18 members of the department won $27 million in the state lottery, January 15, 1995. *Chris Pedota photo*

Ed Colondraes of Clifton, a commercial diver, trails along the rear of a boat as he makes his way back from shore after trying to jack up the bottom of a mule bridge that was crumbling and falling into the Rockaway River, Boonton, May 1999.
Chris Pedota photo

Brig. Gen. James W. Boddie, left, watches as Jim and Caroline Smith of Long Valley unveil a plaque naming Building 65 at Picatinny Arsenal for their son, Cpl. James E. "Jamie" Smith, June 12, 1996. Jamie Smith was killed during the 1993 U.S. mission in Somalia in events later depicted in the film "Black Hawk Down." *Karen Fucito photo*

Pat McConnell, principal biologist for the State Fish, Game and Wildlife Division, holds three 2-month-old bear cubs, April 11, 1993. *Karen Fucito photo*

Stanton Crew's Camaro remains on the Route 80 embankment where he was killed, while police use a metal detector to search for evidence, June 2, 1999. *John Bell photo*

The Stanton Crew Killing

On June 2, 1999, police shot and killed a driver, Stanton Crew, 31, of Morristown, after a short chase from Dover to Parsippany. The resultant investigations centered on whether police were correct in shooting Crew, an African-American, or whether they were guilty of racial profiling and violating his civil rights. In the end, a Morris County grand jury and the U.S. Attorney's Office filed no charges against the officers who shot and killed Crew. "There was no evidence that race influenced the initiation or outcome of the pursuit of Mr. Crew," the office said.

Police said Crew, who was driving with a suspended license, disregarded a signal to pull over from an officer who suspected him of drunken or erratic driving. Carrying a passenger, he headed east from Dover on Route 80 and sideswiped police cruisers before making an abrupt U-turn in Parsippany, veering up an embankment. Authorities maintained Crew nearly ran over officers as they approached his car. Two state troopers, a Denville officer and a Parsippany officer, fired a total of 25 bullets. Four struck Crew.

Crew's mother, sister and brother hired attorney Johnnie Cochran Jr., the celebrated defender of O.J. Simpson. Civil rights activist Al Sharpton also lobbied their cause. The case came to a close in 2002 when the family and Crew's passenger, who was shot in the leg, reached a $1.5 million settlement with Denville, Dover, Parsippany and the state.

Police comb an embankment on westbound Route 80 in Parsippany where driver Stanton Crew of Morristown was shot and killed by police officers after a chase that began in Dover, June 2, 1999. *Chris Pedota photo*

Lillie Crew, mother of shooting victim Stanley Crew looks out of the front door of her home as she is interviewed by reporters, June 1999. *Chris Pedota photo*

Kirby Wall and her grandmother Ollie Wall spoke of the death of their cousin and nephew Stanton Crew, who was shot by police on Route 80 in June 1999. *Chris Pedota photo*

Ingrid Crew, Stanton's sister, Lillie Crew, his mother, and Ollie Wall, his aunt, at the dedication of a memorial to Crew outside his home, June 12, 1999. *Chris Pedota photo*

CELEBRATION

Oomphing marching bands, blaring fire engines, cute little dancing troupes. Have parades never changed?

Memorial Day ceremonies were just as moving 30 years ago as they are today. A St. Patrick's Day parade in Morristown - now Morris County's largest such event - is just as fun, and just as rowdy, as the one it succeeded in Wharton. Fireworks on the Fourth of July were just as spectacular then, as now. Birthdays, weddings, returning home from war are pretty much the same as ever.

One thing was different in these years: Y2K. The close of the 20th century, the arrival of the 21st. The end of a millennium, and, depending on which hype you listened to, the midnight of all sorts of evil things. You were supposed to fill gas tanks before then because beginning at midnight, pumps would no longer work. Bank cards wouldn't spit out cash. Computers (many unable to recognize any year beyond 1999) would freeze up, causing havoc with nearly everything.

None of that happened, of course, in part because the nation spent huge sums to upgrade computers and software. And while many were predicting gloom, others spent 1999 celebrating the great events and important people of the past. A popular question: Who was the most influential person of the last 1,000 years? Answers ran the gamut. As fireworks lit the sky over Morristown's non-alcoholic First Night celebration, we knew one thing: We were ending something, and starting another.

The Colonial Musketeers of Hackettstown march down Ridgedale Avenue as part of the Florham Park parade, July 4, 1997. *Chris Pedota photo*

Park Service members John Dwyer, left, and Steve Klok trek through the snow at Jockey Hollow National Historical Park during a re-enactment of "Washington's Winter." It was one of the bicentennial activities in Morris County, February 21, 1977. George Washington quartered his troops at what is now the park during the winters of 1777 and 1779-80. *Michael Garrney photo*

St. Clare's Harvest Festival, October 1983. *Daily Record staff photo*

Bed races during a festival in Butler, September 29, 1984. *Daily Record staff photo*

"Marching Post" during re-enactment activities celebrating Morris County's bicentennial, January 9, 1977. Washington's Headquarters can be seen in the distance. *John Bell photo*

Mount Tabor Children's Day parade, August 8, 1982. The community's first such parade was held more than 100 years earlier. *Stu Davis Photo*

Boy Scouts from Troop 333 lash tree limbs to make a tower that stood 10 feet high at the Morristown Green, October 10, 1987. From left to right: Parker Jones of Mendham, Aaron Rust of Madison and Stephan Suhocki of Mendham. *Jim Lord photo*

Hay ride participants having a good time during their five-minute journey around the St. Clare's Harvest Festival, Denville, October 13, 1984. The hospital held the big fundraiser for 30 years, with the last being held in 2003.
Daily Record staff photo

Debbie Wolf of Mine Hill is amused that one of her guinea pigs seems to be making a nest in the hair of Kevin Callaghan, a visitor from Belfast, Northern Ireland, July 23, 1987. The two were at Chubb Park in Chester during preparations for a 4-H fair. *Chris Pedota photo*

Rose City festival at Madison High School, June 27, 1987. *Daily Record staff photo*

CELEBRATION

Newlyweds John and Kim Leahy ride in style through County College of Morris after their wedding at Resurrection Parish. They are on the way to the reception at Skylands Restaurant in Randolph, August 1988. *Renee Carolla photo*

Newly trained Santas get ready for the Christmas rush, November 30, 1986. *Daily Record staff photo*

The only remaining section of the once-famous Morris Canal is dedicated in Montville, November 6, 1988. Deputy Mayor Richard Stern and Mayor Frederick E. Eckhardt welcome the first boat to row in the waterway, which was designed to carry coal from the Lehigh Valley to New York harbor. It's the only section of the once-famous waterway, which was completed in 1831, that is still a canal. *Jim Anness photo*

Chris Rea of Mount Tabor sells balloons during a Mount Tabor parade, June 8, 1988. *Jim Lord photo*

Nilam Patel of Parsippany celebrates the Fourth of July after obtaining her citizenship earlier in the year, 1988. She was originally from Guarate, India. *Jim Lord photo*

Brownies march down Route 53 in Denville to start the Denville Christmas parade, November 25, 1989. *Bob Karp photo*

CELEBRATION

Tommy Febick of Mine Hill licks cotton candy off his fingers during the Denville Street Fair, June 11, 1989. *Karen Fucito photo*

Matt Cohen of Rockaway Township downs a watermelon during Rockaway Township Day, August 26, 1989. *Jim Anness photo*

Delores Wilson, president of the Ladies Auxiliary of American Legion Post 390, Denville, and Bill Wagner, also of Post 390, lay flowers at the Civil War monument in a cemetery across from Gardner Field during a Memorial Day ceremony, May 27, 1991.
Karen Fucito photo

The Forbes Magazine balloon team hovers over festivities at the Rockaway Township Day festival, August 26, 1989. *Jim Anness photo*

Nicky Albanito from Troop 145, Mine Hill, folds his neckerchief. He was one of many Boy Scouts who camped out at Schiff Reservation at a Boy Scout Jamboree, October 19, 1991. *Chris Pedota photo*

John Inzilla Jr., a member of the Parsippany High School marching band, plays taps at the end of a Memorial Day service at Vail Cemetery, Parsippany, May 27, 1991. *Bob Karp photo*

American troops during the Revolutionary War re-enactment at Loantaka Park, Morris Township, May 5, 1990. *Tim Farrell photo*

American Legion members of Blue Ridge Post 164 of Hackettstown place flags on veterans' graves on Memorial Day, May 26, 1989. From left to right are Stephen Zeniak, Frank Wirhanowsky, Frank Kilhpaugh and Charles Eshelman. *Daily Record staff photo*

CELEBRATION

Revolutionary War re-enactment in Morris Township, May 20, 1990. *Daily Record staff photo*

American Legion Post 219 Commander Delbert McNeil puts a wreath on a stand during ceremonies at the Lincoln Park post on Memorial Day, May 26, 1991.
Karen Fucito photo

St. Clare's Harvest Festival, Denville, October 7, 1990. *Daily Record staff photo*

Korean War Veteran Earl Hurd, commander of the local Veterans of Foreign Wars, attends a rally during the Persian Gulf War, Randolph, 1991. *Bob Karp photo*

South Street Festival in Morristown as seen from the second floor of the International Pottery building on West Park Street looking down North Park Street. About 20,000 people enjoyed the day, April 5, 1992. *Karen Fucito photo*

A youngster gets a thrill as the tractor lurches at the start of a hay ride at the St. Clare's Harvest Festival in Denville, October 15, 1991. *Bob Karp photo*

CELEBRATION

A woman holds flags during a Memorial Day ceremony on the Green in Morristown, May 31, 1993. *Mike Nixon photo*

Tammi Scalzo of Netcong blows huge bubbles at the Jefferson Day Festival at Jefferson High School, July 11, 1992. *Colleen Harrington photo*

A gymnast from the North Stars in Parsippany does a flip while marching in the Holiday Day Parade in Denville, 1994. *Bob Karp photo*

Clown Tim Tegge greets people arriving at a circus in Denville, May 28, 1995. *Chris Pedota photo*

A Big Bird hugs Christopher Sengal of Landing during a festival at Westbrook Farms in Parsippany, June 2, 1996. *Dawn Benko photo*

Crissie Howell and her brothers, Daniel and Jimmy, of Franklin Township, watch as the Declaration of Independence is read at Washington's Headquarters, Morristown, July 4, 1992. *Chris Pedota photo*

MORRIS COUNTY MEMORIES: VOLUME III

Dana Brannin holds her 10-month-old daughter, Amanda, as the Rev. Martin McDonnell marks the baby's forehead with ashes during Ash Wednesday services at St. Ann Parish in Parsippany, February 22, 1996. *Karen Fucito photo*

Tuba player Darren Large of the Morris Knolls High School marching band plays at halftime of a state championship football game between Morris Knolls and Malcolm X Shabazz High School of Newark, December 8, 1996. *Pierre Van Osten photo*

CELEBRATION

Kathleen Umpstrad, a tiger groom assistant with the Cole Bros. Circus, plays with Dylan, a Siberian tiger cub, Denville, May 28, 1999. *Chris Pedota photo*

Darryl Brushbreaker Jr., a member of the Rosebud Sioux, participates in a powwow at the National Guard Armory in Morris Township, November 25, 1996. *Pierre Van Osten photo*

Morris County celebrates New Year's Eve at the First Night celebration in Morristown, December 31, 1999. *Chris Pedota photo*

Finally, 2000 was really here, during First Night, Morristown, December 31, 1999. *Bob Karp photo*

Boys jump into the Jersey City reservoir from the Washington Street Bridge, Boonton, June 20, 1973. *John Bell Photo*

Boys from Kearney jump into the Jersey City reservoir from the Washington Street Bridge, Boonton, June 19, 1990. *Chris Pedota photo*

RECREATION

Lake Hopatcong sailboat races, June 4, 1977. Fred Eagles hikes out while Bob Aughey steers. *John Bell photo*

Bathers jam the swimming area at Lake Hopatcong, July 19, 1981. *Linda McConnell photo*

Ice-skaters can be seen in the distance on a frozen Lake Parsippany, December 28, 1983. *Daily Record staff photo*

Gabrielle Sodawick going through the course during the Long Valley Rotary Club Horse Show held at Chubb Park, September, 1985. *Daily Record staff photo*

Richard Sommerstein of Livingston drives his 1966 "Amficar" out of Lake Hopatcong in Jefferson, August 14, 1983. *Karen Touhey photo*

RECREATION

Isabelle Elfers tosses a bocce ball down the court while opponents Lillian Farnum and Peg O'Connor look on. They are members of the Senior Bocce Club which meets and plays every Monday and Friday night at the Bocce court at Monroe Hall in Whippany, August, 1993.
Karen Fucito photo

Children cooling off on a hot day at Horseshoe Lake, Roxbury. From left, Frank Smith, Michael Langereis and Dave Freund, July 8, 1982.
Robyn Craig photo

Lifeguard competition at Horseshoe Lake, Roxbury, July 15, 1989. In the far boat is Chris Doran and Kevin Campbell of the Randolph team. In the near boat is Dave Brewster and Amy McCann of the Roxbury team.
Stan Godlewski photo

Ice-skaters enjoy an afternoon on Sunrise Lake, Morris Township, January 4, 1981. *Peter Byron photo*

Marshall Smith and Chelsea Smith at Pleasant Valley pool, May 28, 1985. *Scott Keeler photo*

RECREATION

Slane Hatch cools off his cousin, Justin Paramore, June 16, 1987. *Daily Record staff photo*

Danny MacMahon windsurfing on Lake Parsippany, August 12, 1986.
Stan Godlewski photo

The beach at Lake Hopatcong State Park in Roxbury during a chilly Labor Day, 1994.
Colleen Harrington photo

Bob Burr in "Federal Express" rounds a turn at the state powerboat championships at Lake Hopatcong, September 18, 1994. *Dawn Benko photo*

Morgan Williamson, 6, plays catch with her dog, a Dalamation named Sparky at Lewis Morris Park in Morris Twp. July, 1995. *John Bell photo*

RECREATION

William Wood, 5, from Morristown, makes a stab at a pop up while playing baseball with his brother at the Madison Playground in Madison. August 1995. *Bob Karp photo*

Leigh Odell, Britt Macko, Laura Hockenjos and Meghan Bartley enjoy an afternoon of rollerblading at Loantaka Park in Morris Twp. March 1995. *Bob Karp photo*

Kids cheer on their teammate during the Playground Olympics held at Volunteer Park in Parsippany. Ten Parsippany playgrounds participated. August 1995. *Karen Fucito photo*

PEOPLE

A fair share of famous people lived in, or visited, Morris County from 1970-1999. Former President Reagan loved it for its wealth of big Republican contributors and visited to raise money for his campaigns. Former President Ford came, too. Gov. Tom Kean, another Republican, liked it so much that after leaving office in 1990, he became the 10th president of Drew University in Madison. Millicent Fenwick, the outspoken and sometimes pipe-smoking congresswoman from Bernardsville (and the model for Garry Trudeau's "Doonesbury" character Lacy Davenport), was often in the news before, during and after her four terms in Washington. So was William E. Simon, the former treasury secretary under Presidents Nixon and then Ford, who lived in Harding and contributed so much to charity. Three-term Sen. Bill Bradley lived in Denville.

Normal people were in newspaper pages, too. Like Mamie Truesdale, who died at Morristown Memorial Hospital in 1990 at age 116, according to her figures. Or Sgt. Joseph Walsh of the Morris County Sheriff's Office, who made it to the Guinness Book of World Records as the faster revolver shooter in the mid-1980s.

Morris County was the early home of future TV stars like Gene Shalit, film critic on NBC's "Today" show, who got his start writing a humor column in the Morristown High School newspaper. And to Jane Krakowski (Elaine on "Ally McBeal"), singer Whitney Houston, and stand-up comic Janeane Garofalo, who went to Madison High School. Pittsburgh Steelers quarterback Neil O'Donnell went to the same school.

The county was home to some of the highest wage-earners in the country ... and to a homeless person who sued Morristown and the town's library for mistreatment and won settlements totaling $230,000. To stock car drivers, and airline pilots and inventors with Bell Labs. Doctors, nurses, teachers and athletes.

Gov. Thomas Kean and President Ronald Reagan clasp hands during a presidential fundraiser in Parsippany, October 4, 1985. *Karen Touhey photo*

Rep. Millicent Fenwick at a re-election victory party, Bernardsville, June 8, 1982. The pipe-smoking, four-term GOP congresswoman from Bernardsville was first elected in 1974 at the age of 64. Some say she was the model for the character of Lacey Davenport in Garry Trudeau's popular comic strip "Doonesbury." *Dave Schemelia photo*

William E. Simon, right, U.S. treasury secretary under President Ford from 1974-77, with friends Ettore Barbatelli and William Lanigan, November 6, 1986. Simon, who lived in Harding, made a fortune in leveraged buyouts. *Daily Record staff photo*

Mamie Truesdale at age 108, July 18, 1982.
Robert S. Townsend photo

Mamie Truesdale at age 111, September 11, 1984.
Daily Record staff photo

Centenarian claimed to be 116

Mamie Truesdale became something of a Morris County celebrity during her lifetime, which was considerably long by anyone's account.

If you go by "Grandma" Truesdale's calculations, she was 116 when she died August 24, 1990, at Morristown Memorial Hospital. There was no way to verify her date of birth. There were no official records, just her memories of the past. But according to government records, she was more likely 106 or 107 years old, which still made her one of New Jersey's oldest residents.

Truesdale was interviewed by the Daily Record many times during the 47 years she lived on Clyde Potts Drive in Morristown, and during the last five years of her life at Morris View nursing home in Morris Township. The granddaughter of an African slave, she claimed she was born in 1873. She began picking cotton as soon as she was able. She later worked on a South Carolina peanut farm, fished as often as she could and chewed tobacco from the time she was 12 — a habit she maintained throughout her life.

In 1900 she married Chalmus Truesdale and then had nine children. When her husband died in 1943, she moved to Morristown to be with her daughter, sister and granddaughter. She worked as a presser in a laundry for 38 years before retiring in 1952.

Truesdale said in a 1985 interview that one of her biggest disappointments in life was not learning to read or write well. But two years later she had learned her multiplication tables and received an honorary degree from Morristown High School.

Mamie Truesdale at age 113, September 6, 1986.
Daily Record staff photo

Actress Maureen O'Hara talks with Frank Burke, owner of the Quiet Man in Dover, November 9, 1985. The restaurant is named for the 1952 movie "The Quiet Man" about a disgraced American boxer who retires to Ireland, where he finds love. O'Hara stared in the movie with John Wayne. *Jeff Gottlieb photo*

Sister Mary Urban, president of the board of trustees at St. Clare's Hospital in Denville, helps Stephanie Bindas of Boonton with a display for the hospital's October 1983 Harvest Festival.

Lois Frank of Mendham, left, widow of Morris Frank, a founder of The Seeing Eye, with Bonnie Lanzet and guide dog Zabrina. Zabrina was the 10,000th dog trained by The Seeing Eye, and Bonnie was her recipient, January 16, 1991. *Karen Fucito photo*

Rep. Millicent Fenwick of Bernardsville, former President Gerald Ford and Rep. Jim Courter of Hackettstown at a press conference. *Daily Record staff photo*

Sgt. Joseph Walsh of the Morris County Sheriff's Office demonstrates the proper shooting stance to the other officers, October 9, 1977. A firearms instructor for 30 years, he was listed in the 1986 Guinness Book of World Records as the fastest draw in the world. His skill earned him an appearance on the "Late Night With David Letterman" show. *John Bell photo*

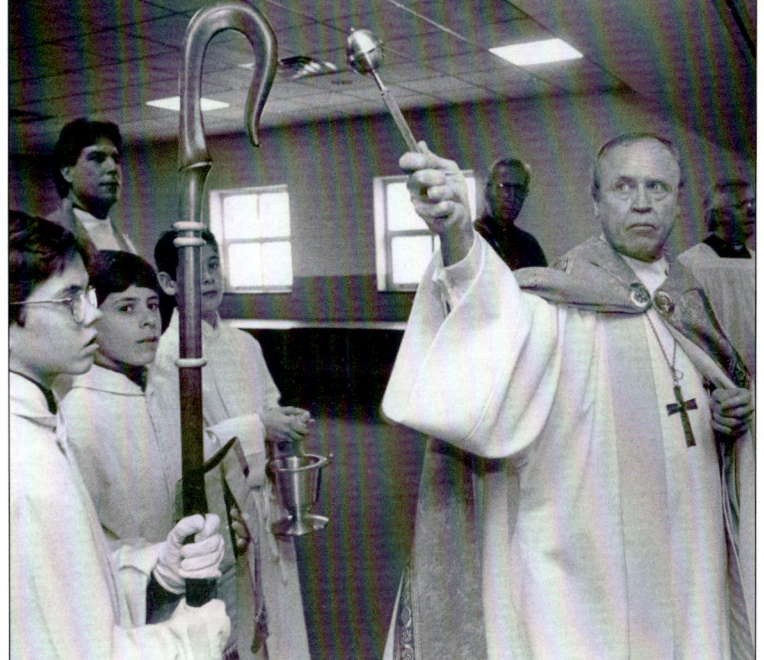

Bishop Frank J. Rodimer of the Roman Catholic Diocese of Paterson blesses the conference room of the new St. Patrick's Parish Center in Chatham, January 14, 1990. *Bob Karp photo*

PEOPLE

New Jersey Gov. Thomas Kean signs a bill buying 80 acres of land to save Pyramid Mountain in Boonton and Kinnelon from developers. With him are Assemblyman Alex DeCroce, left, Assemblymen Bob Martin, Kinnelon Mayor Glenn Sisco, State Sen. Leanna Brown and Lucy Meyer, chairwoman of the Committee to Save Pyramid Mountain, Kinnelon, August 4, 1989. *Realf Schermer photo*

Former New Jersey Gov. Tom Kean, president of Drew University, poses for a portrait in Mead Hall after its reconstruction from a fire in 1989, Madison, 1993. *Karen Fucito photo*

Kean Becomes President of Drew

Nearly 5,000 people from around the country witnessed the two-hour inauguration on April 20, 1990, of former Gov. Thomas H. Kean as Drew University's 10th president. The ceremony took place under a huge white tent at the Madison campus. During the opening remarks of his inauguration speech, Kean said: "Nine presidents have preceded me to this wooded land...as I resume the responsibilities of the presidency, I am awed by these mighty oaks of Drew's past. I pray that I may honor their memory by leading Drew to its finest days." As governor (he served two four-year terms from 1982-1990), Kean had been a dedicated proponent of public education excellence. Prior to becoming an elected official, he had taught history and government at St. Mark's, a Massachusetts preparatory school that he attended, and political science at Rutgers University. Kean ended his address by vowing to turn Drew — a microcosm of America's future, he said – into a melting pot of ideas where student ethnic diversity could help chop down the wilderness of criticism that had haunted American universities during the past few years. *Compiled by Janine Mellini.*

Chatham High School's Billy Walsh, right, reacts after scoring the decisive goal in a semifinal state championship soccer game, November 6, 1993. Teammate Steve Pignatello cheers, too. Walsh went on to play on Olympic and professional teams. *Karen Fucito photo*

PEOPLE

Bishop Frank J. Rodimer leads about 500 people in prayer during an protest in front of medical offices where abortions were performed in Morristown, October 31, 1992.
Chris Pedota photo

MORRIS COUNTY MEMORIES: VOLUME III

VIEWS FROM AROUND THE COUNTY

Maybe it's because they're so photogenic, but the young are favorites of photographers. Looking around Morris County, Daily Record photographers usually found them.

We saw them skateboarding in 1978 and snowboarding in 1999. Picking dandelions in Morristown and picking pumpkins in Randolph. Studying hard at school in Parsippany and wrestling with rudimentary computers in Morris Plains in 1981. Slurping ice cream cones in Denville and celebrating Randolph High School's miracle comeback victory in a state championship football game against Montclair High School in 1990.

Some scenes in the following pages feature adults, and some may look like something like you saw just yesterday - common occurrences like an overturned truck on Route 287, cars rounding the Morristown Green in 1979, a full moon over Lake Parsippany.

Others appear quaint, at least by today's standards – even something so "modern" as Bell Labs staffers playing chess against a computer in Morris Township ... in 1983. At the time, it was different!

Cory Wall, 4, Christopher Wall, 6, and Kim DiPietro, 7, enjoy a ride on the tire swing at the Jefferson Twp. Municipal playground. June 1995. *Chris Pedota photo*

VIEWS FROM AROUND THE COUNTY

Crossroads at the Morristown Green, June 27, 1973. *John Bell photo*

Columbia Road looking west from Normandy Parkway intersection, Morris Township, circa 1970. *Daily Record staff photo*

Section of Morris Canal, Boonton. Little is left of the canal, and someone had dropped this debris there, August 10, 1974. *Bruce Crawford photo*

Archaeological excavation site being surveyed in Parsippanny, October 14, 1973. *Daily Record staff photo*

Aerial view of Morristown, showing the Green, bottom left, and the excavation for Headquarters Plaza, October 14, 1974. *Daily Record staff photo*

VIEWS FROM AROUND THE COUNTY

Route 46 looking east in Rockaway Township, April 26, 1977. *Bruce Crawford photo*

Frelinghuysen Mansion, February 8, 1975. The summer home of George and Sara Frelinghuysen was given to Morris County after their deaths. It is now the headquarters of the Morris County Park Commission. The Morris Township home is on the National Register of Historic Places. *Bruce Crawford photo*

Student Howard Herrick holds his head in frustration at Parsippany High School, March 22, 1979. *Daily Record staff photo*

Joe Congdon, left, and Kenneth Thomspon, scientists at Bell Labs, in Morris Township, November 1983. *Stan Godlewski photo*

Nicole Jurecky in the reading area at a Montessori school in Parsippany, July 18, 1980. *Robyn Craig photo*

Businesses on North Park Place adjacent to the Green, Morristown, December 29, 1979. *Stu Davis photo*

VIEWS FROM AROUND THE COUNTY

Kathy Kahn, left, and Stacy Warner pick wildflowers at Pleasant Valley Park, June 11, 1985. *Daily Record staff photo*

Boy Scout Jamboree at the Schiff Reservation, Mendham Township, 1985. *Daily Record staff photo*

Students at a computer camp class in Morris Plains, June 29, 1981. *John Bell photo*

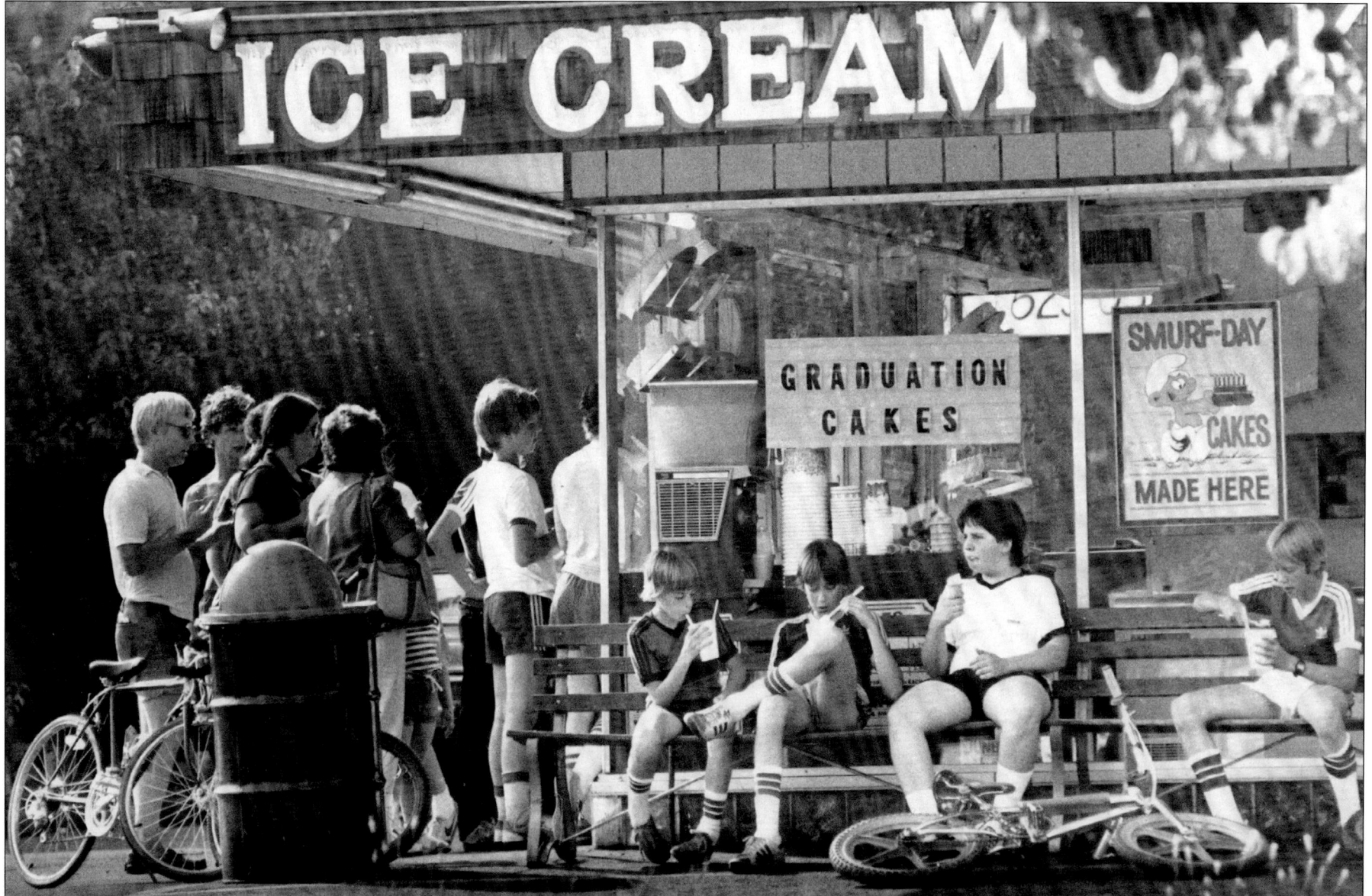

What better way to cool off than with a soda or ice cream cone. Left to right, sitting on bench in Denville: Richard and David Wolter of Mountain Lakes, Brett Seitz of Parsippany and Larry Page of Mountain Lakes, June 11, 1984. *N.R. Rowan photo*

VIEWS FROM AROUND THE COUNTY

LaNiece Bouldin jumps in a round of double dutch with the rope swung by Tanemka Keys, left, and Hope Samuels, Morristown, August 20, 1987. *Karen Fucito photo*

Tyrone King of Morristown, a member of the breakdance group called "Fresh" of Morristown, gives a demonstration at the Morris County Mall, Hanover, February 16, 1984.
Scott Keeler photo

Alexander Ostrowski on his scooter in Hanover, November 5, 1987.
Daily Record staff photo

Motorists are advised about a potential goose crossing by the Harding municipal building, August 11, 1986. The geese enjoyed a pond by the Church of Christ the King across the road. *Glen E. Ellman photo*

Skateboarders show off their talents at Family Day celebration, 1978.
Daily Record staff photo

VIEWS FROM AROUND THE COUNTY

Bryan Mortenson of Morris Township picks dandelions along Washington Street in Morristown, May 8, 1986. *Karen Toubey photo*

Red skies at night usually mean that the next day is going to be a hot one, Lake Parsippany, July 11, 1988. *Jim Anness photo*

A state police officer fills out a report that will start the investigation of an overturned pickup on Route 287, January 1988. *Chris Pedota photo*

A daughter helps her father bring in pumpkins from the field to be sold at the Knoth family farm stand on Millbrook Avenue, Randolph, October 1985. *Daily Record staff photo*

Swinging on a tree in their front yard are Jeanette Dewit, her brother Joshua and their friend Michele Driesse, Pompton Plains, March 25, 1987. *Karen Fucito photo*

Boys enjoy a late afternoon swim at the Mine Hill Beach, July 11, 1988.
Karen Fucito photo

Matt Danbar throws a rock into Indian Lake, Denville, May 18, 1989.
Karen Fucito photo

VIEWS FROM AROUND THE COUNTY

Whippany Park High School pitcher Toni Fortunato is mobbed by teammates after their softball team won the Morris County Tournament, November 1990.
Dawn Benko photo

Shakil, Aqueel and Haroon Chaudhry of Boonton play on the jungle gym at Grace Lord Park, November 5, 1988. *Jim Anness photo*

Kevin Mohr (foreground) of Roxbury leaves the blocks in the 100-meter butterfly in a coed swim meet against Parsippany. He won easily and his team splashed to a 53-33 victory against the Redskins.
Karen Fucito photo

Spectators play during halftime of a homecoming football game at Delbarton School, Morris Township, October 1993. *Bob Karp photo*

VIEWS FROM AROUND THE COUNTY

Children play on a hammock on Juniper Drive, Morris Plains, May 23, 1991.
Bob Karp photo

Firemen from the New Jersey Firemen's Home in Boonton. Behind Edward Dyer, center, are former chief Ed Russell, left, Howard Conn, William Lucas and Luigi Scerbo. Behind the firemen is the 1915 American LaFrance horse-drawn steamer.
Daily Record staff photo

Boys show their stuff at Burnham Park pool, Morristown, July 19, 1990.
Bob Karp photo

A bicyclist heads up Parsippany Road during the height of a rainstorm, Parsippany, May 7, 1991. *Chris Pedota photo*

Roy Hilderbrant and one of his wolf dogs, Cody, on their front porch in Hackettstown, 1992. *Bob Karp photo*

VIEWS FROM AROUND THE COUNTY

Nicole Oliveri, left, Lorissa Bertolini and Lauren Oliveri enjoy an afternoon at Memorial Park pool, Morris Township, July 7, 1993. *Karen Fucito photo*

Robin Friebur, Laya Bautista and Jesse Friebur venture out on a tree limb over Loantaka Brook, Convent Station, November 15, 1993. *Dawn Benko photo*

Brian Elko of Morris Knolls High School wins the backstroke at a White Meadow Lake Swim meet, Rockaway Township, 1995.

Bob Karp photo

Luke Hatcher has a grand time on the Mount Olive Municipal Beach, Budd Lake, June 25, 1993.
Tim Farrell photo

Morristown National Little League 11-year-old All Stars celebrate a 1-0 victory over rival Par-Troy East, 1994. In the center of the pile is winning pitcher Kimber Auerbach. *Karen Fucito photo*

Lightning seen from the Montville Township Community Center complex on Changebridge Road, June 29, 1994. This is a time-lapse photo of about two minutes at an aperture of F8. The double line running diagonally through the lightning bolts are from the lights of an airplane. *Dawn Benko photo*

VIEWS FROM AROUND THE COUNTY

Sister Elaine, a Carmelite nun, shovels the walk in front of the Carmel Convent, Morris Township, February 3, 1996. *Bob Karp photo*

Morristown High School's Devon George competes in the backstroke leg of the 200-meter individual medley against Morris Knolls High School, January 19, 1996. *Bob Karp photo*

Maryann Newman ventures through the Drew University campus with her dog, Max, after a snowstorm, Madison, January 23, 1998. *Bob Karp photo*

Boonton High School heavyweight wrestler Joe Franc lets loose a primal scream after pinning his opponent, 1997. *Chris Pedota photo*

Dave Mills of West Milford heads out to an afternoon of ice fishing in the Great Cove section of a frozen Lake Hopatcong, Mount Arlington, January 28, 1999. *Chris Pedota photo*

VIEWS FROM AROUND THE COUNTY

Randolph High School quarterback and kicker Mike Groh (13) after hitting a 37-yard field goal with 1 second left to win a state championship football game against Montclair High School, December 1990. *Bob Karp photo*

Utility poles brought down by a heavy coating of ice on Salmon Road, Roxbury, February 5, 1998. *Chris Pedota photo*

Ryan Hall of Landing snowboarding over a ramp at Hopatcong State Park, Roxbury, March 16, 1999. *Dawn Benko photo*